White Papers

PITT POETRY SERIES
Ed Ochester, Editor

ollins, Martha, 1940–
hite papers /

2012.
33053225295264
i   05/02/12

PAPERS

MARTHA COLLINS

University of Pittsburgh Press

Published by the University of Pittsburgh Press, Pittsburgh, Pa., 15260

Copyright © 2012, Martha Collins

All rights reserved

Manufactured in the United States of America

Printed on acid-free paper

10 9 8 7 6 5 4 3 2 1

ISBN 13: 978-0-8229-6184-0

ISBN 10: 0-8229-6184-9

for Mary Alice Mathews

White Papers

Because my father said *Yes*
but not in our lifetimes Because
my mother said *I know my daughter*
would never <u>want</u> to marry . . .

But mostly because they rarely spoke
of or noticed or even whispered
about and did not of course . . .

Because magazines rarely TV
rarely textbooks rarely or not
at all except for figures like
George Washington Carver
who'd lived in our state

Because among the crayons
there was one called Flesh

Because paintings rarely or never
until because books from the library
never *until* because college literature
not at all the American lit anthology
had only Gwendolyn Brooks
who was not assigned

Because a few years after Brown
v. Board of Education I wrote a paper
that took the position *Yes but not yet*

the skin under
all skin is all
white seen skin
is skin deep none

is white pink
is blood showing
through almost
transparent thin

skin blood as in
on our hands
protected by gloves
laws guns while

brown tan to almost
black protects from
sun that burns
us red-handed us

[3]

they lived

in the colored section
of town though we lived

in a city not a town it had
a downtown where we saw

them sometimes in stores
on streets at the movies we

didn't think much about
it did we lived in Iowa where

we saw them mostly saw
ourselves what did

we didn't know
where we were living

[4]

In the dream I am black, telling myself, who am white,
who I am. Like the woman inside the man, or like

the man inside the woman the man who wrote
about these things found hard to handle I

wrote:
anima soul
animus soul or

skin was black but her heart
was white she wrote of herself I

wrote *that was white*
of you they said *black*

step back hide inside
anima animus animal's

all of us but *soul*

you know is black

black keys letters learn
to play read write dress
shoes purse suit grown
up clothes hat tie night
out morning coffee not
yet sin will find you out
dirt sheep eye and blue
mark so it seemed wrong
that *in the* meant good
book word confused with
Middle English *blāc* pale
(see *bleach*) oh no never

They lived *in the colored*
section of town, as if the White
Pages map had been crayoned,
little squares, inside the lines,

as if they too had been covered
with color, something added to what
was given, i.e. ourselves who did
not know, not even our teachers,

that they were the given, that we
were the altered, that we (who still
were they, there was no difference
yet) lost our color, slowly erased

it as we moved north where a distant
sun could not get through, and on
we went, making roads and maps
of rivers and roads, assuming

we owned it if we could draw
it and color it in and give it
a name, and still we are drawing
lines and calling them borders

and coloring in and naming
people who shall not must
not cross, who live in the colored
sections of our white minds.

white line broken line white dividing
right from right white sign house oh

New England white church white
meetinghouse on green commons

where slaves could not stroll at night
in Boston carry sticks or canes

where African slaves were first bought
with Pequots captured in *Just warre*

where slaves were sometimes sold in taverns

where churches bought them for ministers

where ministers lawyers doctors farmers
used them for cutting carting hoeing
husking mowing ferrying carrying

and where in any case the slave trade . . .

where the last slave died in 1859 in Rhode Island

oh New England your white meeting broken oh

Not mine: mine came late
they lived in England

which supplied more slave
ships sold more slaves than all
the colonies and states combined

Not mine: mine came late
and poor from Ireland
from which servants
and virtual slaves

but which also supplied
crews and which for sugar

Not mine: mine came late
they lived in Wales

which supplied copper for shackles
and ships and besides they came not
so late to South Carolina where

Not mine: mine came late
from German Switzerland

Not mine: mine came late
from Germany *which*

New England food to the West Indies for
    sugar molasses back to New England
        distilled into rum to Africa for
slaves for West Indies plantations for

            50 gallons rum = 1 man in prime

Ships built in owned by captained
    by crewed by New England to Africa for
        slaves for the South for naval supplies
to New England for ships to Africa for

            Brown University / Faneuil Hall

In 1808 the slave trade was abolished
    but not ended: still New England its white
        captains' merchants' bankers' houses because

        In what year did Eli Whitney invent the cotton gin?
  How did this invention affect American commerce and industry?

Food south for cotton north for
    textiles south as *negro cloth* for
        cotton north for textiles south
and east to Britain for goods for

           New England / where I live . . .

two back then who lived in my aunt's

big house he cleaned she cooked none

at home till neighbors brought their own

one from Mississippi none in my grade

school none in church this doesn't

count my not-quite gold-skinned

made-up flowered lived in the jungle

or maybe the swamp we pricked

our fingers mixed our blood in a dark

space in my ten-year-old mind then

one in junior high but not in my class

one in high school but not—

except for not-quite her I didn't . . .

but oh I knew how many oh yes I knew

Black Codes (from *code noir*)
restricted blacks in southern states
after the Civil War but in midwestern states
before the War including Iowa where . . .

Slavery was illegal in first the territory, then the state,

> *but black persons could not move to Iowa*
> *without a Certificate of Freedom and a $500 bond.*

The Underground Railroad ran across Iowa, west to east,

> *but black persons were prohibited from voting, attending*
> *white schools, serving in the militia or legislature,*
> *testifying against or marrying white persons.*

After the Civil War, Iowa was the _____ state to pass civil
rights legislation.   (*fourth*)

In 1948, _____ sued Katz Drug Store in Des Moines
for refusing to serve her ice cream.   (*Edna Griffin*)

Mr. Katz, earlier acquitted three times for similar charges,
was convicted of violating the _____ civil rights act.   (*1884*)

I remember Mr. Katz.

I did not learn about Black Codes.

Five white baby dresses

Milk in glass bottles, cream on top

Sheets on beds, lines, beds

Snow window snow

His white handkerchief, our white gloves

His starched white shirt, even at home

Gray faces framed in white

Black faces in negatives

Shadows in the sidewalk's gray mirror

The Shadow knows

New coloring books, grown-up books without pictures

White keys first, then the harder black

Frost on the window, breath in the air

Chalk, eraser, chalk on the board:

Black page for white words

                              Water filling the white tub

                              Layers of white lingerie

                              Dress train cap veil

                              White-ribboned candles, knife

Our first big wars were white
wars, as far as we knew from school,
which left out most native Americans
and all native Africans, slave and free.

Our first world war was also
white, as far as we knew from school,
which left out India and Africa, even
the Middle East, which at the time was also

white, as Jesus was white,
but which seems less so in our current
wars, which have some roots in that first
world war, see *Iraq, British creation of*, see *Palestine*,

British Mandate for: see *Churchill 1922*, see *1939*,
among the most famous white papers in the world.

this is a white on white

paper if you are finding

it hard to read white

words on white consider

a white on white shirt

bleached laundered

starched buttoned

up collared no colored

stripes just white lines no

stars except in a white

sky no clash a little

glare perhaps but nothing

rising up off the page

black keys from trees white keys locked

on black shoulders locked together above

skeleton ribs keys to 45 keyboards from one

tusk *the word ivory rang through the air*

one tusk + one slave to carry it bought

together if slave survived the long march

sold for spice or sugar plantations if not

replaced by other slaves five Africans died

for each tusk 2 million for 400,000 American

pianos including the one my grandmother

played not to mention grieving villages

burned women children left to die the dead

elephants whose tusks went to Connecticut

where they were cut bleached and polished

while my grandmother played in Illinois

my mother played and I— there were many old

pianos and slaves were used till the 20th century:

an African slave could have carried a tusk

that was cut into white keys I played, starting

with middle C and going up and down

In My Toybox / On My Bookshelf

Raggedy Ann   Raggedy Andy
Beloved Belindy

Beloved Belindy was the mammy of Raggedy Ann and Raggedy Andy and of all the other dolls in the nursery. She was the nicest, fattest, soft rag doll you would ever care to cuddle. And the smile painted on her broad face was as cheery as could be. One just has to be happy, when one wears a happy smile, or else the smile will soon go away. But when a smile is painted on, it is almost certain never to come off . . .

and then when they couldn't afford
it but they did afford it they hired
Cecil to wash iron clean once a week
my mother picked her up and took
her back to the colored section of town
and once she had my mother to lunch
with her friends and sometimes they
prayed together including the day
before my wedding for which she served
the reception although she also came
to the service we all loved her loved
her wisdom I loved her beautiful crown
of braids who knows what she felt what
did I know about her ask her first name

[this page blank]

Of course there were browns
who weren't black, but we called
them white or didn't call them
or know them, except for Señor
Briseño who taught Spanish.

No one was Latin American then
or Hispanic or Latino, although
we'd heard a name for Mexicans,
and also one for Italians, who lived
in their own section of town.

Of course there were the confusing
other Indians, one of whom my mother
knew: a pastor's wife who wore a sari
so people wouldn't think she
was, you know, what she wasn't.

My mother had a Lebanese friend
who went to our church, but no
one was Arab or Muslim then,
or terrorist, only Communist: our
Other did not live among us except

of course for African Americans,
who were still called Negro or colored,
who were not many in our city but
were just enough to be other than
whatever it was we were.

STARK WHITE AND
COLONIAL KHAKI RULE
THE URBAN JUNGLE
            —*Elle*, April 2008

The British brought
khaki to India, dyed
their summer whites

The American army
copied in 1898 our
first colonial war

and afterward until
we went to the jungle
and copied trees

There is no jungle
in this our first
largely urban war

In this war our letter
stamps became flags
waving on khaki

Why don't
you wear a flag
pin they asked one

of our candidates
who often wears
white shirts

which look quite nice
against his khaki
American skin

not black
almost black
brown tan
beige white as

        brown
        often brown
        often tan
        beige white as

                not red
                maybe paint
                brown tan
                beige white as

        not yellow
        yellow under-
        tones tan
        beige white as

not white
beige pink
burned red
tanned tan as

[19]

Before *white* meant
masters though not
long before it meant

settlers, i.e. white-
not-native came before
white-not-[black]-slave

share
stake
claim

Indians got to wear feathers
(had a headdress with many
of many colors) but
cowgirls carried cap guns
(had two) and always won.

paleface   face seen

redskin   not faced

The Lone Ranger on a white
horse could not be (a)lone

and still be our American-
story hero but Tonto
of course meant—

Well we didn't
know: Kemo Sabe
was *¿quién sabe?* we
heard in Spanish along
with *tonto* (adjective) stupid

Wapsipinicon Nishnabotna
Pottawattamie Chickasaw

rivers counties even
our state for the Ioway
tribe long gone now

only the once removed
returned Meskwaki I never
went to their annual powwow

the Massachusetts
most of them dead of disease before
the Pilgrims named this now my state

our first "providential" plague

the hundreds of Pequots
men women and children burned alive
in their village or slain escaping in 1637

our first war

the natives of southern New England
most of them gone by 1700

our first them

red apple wagon fire-
truck haul the long over
the sea parting the waves
this letter day ribbon
stop *skin* we said paint
the town were you ever
scare blood on my skirt
stop we said by whatever
means to end to move
them war war no skin
so red perhaps not skin but
what spilled from inside it

Children's Song #1

Jesus loves the little children,
All the children of the world.
Red and yellow, black and white,
They are precious in His sight.
Jesus loves the little children of the world.

Children's Song #2, as sung

The poor old slave has gone to rest,
We know that he is free.
His bones they lie, disturb them not,
Way down in Tennessee.

The pee-oor old slee-ave . . .

The piggity-poor old sliggity-slave . . .

Children's Song #3

My heart was black with sin
Until the Savior came in.
His precious blood, I know,
Has washed it white as snow.

In the usually black but sometimes
red ("it *should* be read") Bible,
our sins are scarlet before
they are white as snow,

not, as in the hymn, black
with sin before washed
in blood, made white
as snow (always *snow*).

In the Bible, lepers are white
before singers are dressed
in white linen, before many
are purified and made white.

Is there any taste in the white
of an egg? asks Job.

An angel came upon
them from the realms
heard on high, but only

after He was transfigured
in raiment white as the light
and crucified and resurrected

did an angel appear in white.

Renaissance angels were often dressed
in brown, ochre, rose, even green
or blue, except the baby angels
who were not dressed at all.

American angels, especially
Christmas angels, are almost
always dressed in white.

In the vision of the last days,
His head and hair are white
like wool (yes wool, He
is the lamb), white as snow:

a white horse a white throne
white angels white-robed multitudes

and armies clothed in white
riding white horses

to make turn grow become
white, sea with foam, skin with

white lead + chalk
white lead + mercury
white lead + arsenic
white lead + vinegar*

Egypt to Greece to Rome
to Italy Spain France England

where ceruse* was used by Queen
Elizabeth for smallpox scars, but

it was also "The Mask of Youth,"
and see *Poetry, Renaissance*

marble milk lilies snow
see *Shakespeare*: nothing like

eggshells egg whites ass's milk
bled with leeches lancets cups

to whiten
what we now
say is whiteness

The Irish were not, the Germans
were not, the Jews Italians Slavs and others
were not, or were not exactly or not quite
at various times in American history.

Before us the Greeks themselves
were not (though the weaker enemy
Persians were), the next-up Romans
themselves were not either.

And later the Europeans were not
until Linnaeus named by color,
red white yellow and black.

Even the English settlers were only
vaguely at first, to contrast with natives,
but then, with Africans, more and more
of them slaves to be irreversibly,
totally different from, they were.

Then others were not, then were,
or were not, but gradually became,
leaving only, for a time, black
and yellow to be not.

Then there were other words
for those who were still or newly
(see *immigrant*, *Arab*) somehow not
the same and therefore not.

Thus history leaves us nothing
but not: like children playing at being
something, we made, we keep
making our whiteness up.

My class in my all-white school
had just one Catholic, one Jew.
In junior high, someone new:
a Japanese American girl
born like us a year before
Pearl Harbor, before internment.
Her family lived in our section
of town, but were they there
before, or had they fled the West
before, or after, was she maybe one
of the hundred and ten thousand, did
she remember fences wire the war
we didn't remember, we didn't
know much about her, who wasn't us—

The first wars of my life
were Asian wars, including
half of the one I don't remember.

registered curfewed restricted removed
from *military areas* (e.g., the Pacific Coast)
to fairgrounds racetracks stables and then

interned on land *raw and untamed but full*
of opportunity where they slept on cots
in tarpaper barracks worked went to school

made in fear of
the possible German
but used against

August 1945

The first war I remember began
the day I went to summer camp.

That fall we studied Communism
and found Korea's finger on the map.

The monosyllabic names
for our Asian enemies had

more bite than *Commie*
or *Ruskie* with their *—ies*

though there was *Charlie*

Not just My Lai but also Operation Speedy Express
in which thousands mostly civilians (found few guns)
were killed for *the body count* if they ran or did or were

Protests marches teach-ins sit-ins I tried to write
a poem a woman walked across a field across
my mind *does she carry a gun / I do not know*

And later I went to Vietnam *It will change your life*
my friend said *I do not know—Tôi không biết—*
I did not know, but they taught me

no Chinatown in my hometown just
missionary chopstick news we knew
that San Francisco had we didn't
know the gold rush brought

them maybe knew the trans-
continental railroad brought we
didn't know when it was done the Act
of 1882 excluded though women still

were bought to yes until the war
we knew when it wasn't China it
was Japan this was years before I rode
the train to a school near San Francisco built

by one of the rich railroad men my large
class had a few Asian Americans I knew one

a few white tulips with slender petals
    but mostly colored: magenta pink-
        streaked yellow red

imported of course from Holland where
    fortunes were made and lost
        on the most exotic

but first from Afghanistan
    Turkey Iran their name
        the Turkish word for *turban*

an item worn by some of our current
    Other: formerly seen as more
        or less white but recently un-

whitened colored not to be bought
    and sold but made by other
        means to do our bidding

white   money   much
money   most   money
white   money   means
money   free   money
white   money   mine

"Your paycheck when it's signed by a white man."
www.urbandictionary.com

slaves hoeing picking bailing
carrying loading trundling cotton

butchering hogs mining mowing
men women children families

It's right on the money, said
John W. Jones, the black artist

who made paintings of the slave
images featured on southern currency

that was printed until the Civil War
in Boston New York Philadelphia

including also the goddess of money
with slaves in cotton fields behind:

white cotton gold coins black
faces hands white money

"Let me see the color of your money."

in front of a store

whistled or spoke or

$4,000 paid by *Look*

so we know they said

they beat him shot him

in Money, Mississippi

"We established White Money
to make life easier for business persons."
www.whitemoney.com

white	money	white
paper	white	my
white	papers	white

could get a credit card loan car

come and go without a never had

to think about a school work job

to open doors to buy a rent a nice

place yard park beside a walk

in any store without a never had

to dress to buy a dress shoes under-

wear to understate or -play myself

to make myself heard to get across

a street a never mind point I never

had to earn the right to make

my way if I should lose my way or

all I own my open door world was all

before me where to choose to and I

[this page blank]

paper sheets of sheets
robes of hoods winking
clouds stirring storm

coming home to front
door closing back to back
to roost pigeons whitened

doves among white
blossoms trees limbs
swaying eyes gleaming

teeth bones remaining
dangling fleshless white
bodies underneath after all

In a place where things occurred they keep occurring.

In Cairo, for instance, in southern Illinois.

from an arch with a clothesline rope 1909
from a wire mesh ceiling 1967
with his shoelaces 2005

arrested   jailed   not white

LYNCHING reported thousands

SUICIDE declared *in view of*
the current turmoil despite evidence

SUICIDE declared despite confusion regarding
two pairs of shoes and the city attorney's opinion that
this was not a suicide or a homicide. There are things in between.

As in the mind, where things that occurred keep occurring.

As in the state of, as in the United States.

sale sheets
on the line sails
in the sunset
towns where black

could not be seen
after dark there
were other towns
where yellow could

not later not Jew there
were signs lettered
on wood scratched
on absence there

were numbers some
then none by ban
decree threat attack:
a price for living

in or staying past
a long day of work
burning crosses white
sheets turned against

a dark sky the coming
in of the kept out
in the wind waves
of whites only within

city limits after dark
whites only under
the stones no skin
covering

The Illinois town where my parents met was not an all-white "sundown" town, although such towns, including the county seat, were all around them.

There, the year before they were born, Ruby Berkley Goodwin was born on, yes, the other side of town, but among Irish, German, and other immigrants.

Like my father's father, her father worked in the mines, went on strike with the miners' union, ran up debt in the company store.

Her family also lived in a small house with two coal stoves, knew the same doctors, bottling company, grocers.

Like my father, Ruby's cousin went to work in a local drugstore instead of the mines.

Every year, in the opera house, they all saw *Uncle Tom's Cabin* (on stage, then on film), though no one ever called my mother Topsy.

And of course they went to different churches, and Ruby went to the colored high school, whose students, my mother said, came to the white school for science labs, which was *all they ever asked for*, which I know from Ruby's book is not true.

Nor, I think, did my parents hear stories of southern chain gangs and other post-Reconstruction re-enslavements.

But after she had taught, worked as a journalist, finished college, served as Hattie McDaniel's publicist (she would later act herself), and published poems,

Ruby wrote *It's Good to Be Black*, about growing up in Du Quoin,

and mentioned my mother's father, who printed in his newspaper only the *nice things that happened among the Negroes,*

giving me a connection to the other side of the town

where my parents lived in not-quite-all-whiteness.

In the famous first [part-] talkie film, a black
-faced white man sings white songs called "jazz"

Black-faced, he looks in the mirror
and sees his cantor father canting

Gray-faced, he mouths words
to a paler girl we never hear

White words on a black screen
with quotation marks, elaborate dashes

Black-faced, backstage, in black undershirt:
"He talks like Jakie ~ but he looks like his shadow."

Pale mouth, songs coming out
White shirt, white gloves

Gray-faced, he sings for his dying father
"Your papa is so sick ~ his face is so pale ~~"

Black-faced, for his mother, *My little
Mammy*, whose lips he's kissed

(fade to white shirt)

and if I look at your face at your hands your
triumphant or suffering body and do not
see, if the mirror neurons that make
me experience another's actions
as my own do not fire

who wasn't us
who isn't us
who isn't there

I may find in your face
my father my mother my most
desired despised my most from even
myself hidden other myself displaced not re-
cognized and you of course defaced your self erased

to make turn grow become
black darken denigrate sully
air with smoke, skin with

burnt cork
boot polish
greasepaint

On stage: Mr. Tambo Mr. Bones tambourines
castanets danced joked got to mock insult
humiliate violate make a travesty of but
also got to say what could not say too
lewd taboo insinuate regress let out
the old repressed could hate *and*
love embrace it's easy to turn

"the very pinks of Negro singers"
        —NY *Herald*, 1848, on Christy Minstrels

On screen: all or some of the
blacks in all nine versions
of *Uncle Tom's Cabin,* all
in *The Birth of a Nation*

Al Jolson playing himself
Judy Garland & Mickey Rooney
Bing Crosby in *Holiday Inn*, which
also gave us "White Christmas"
      [1903–1927, 1915, 1927, 1939, 1942]

In our Girl Scout show, my best friend,
our Mr. Interlocutor, was dressed
in a boy's white suit; the rest
of us wore old clothes. Our end
men Bones and Tambo spoke
some dialect, told bad jokes;
the rest of us sang or danced . . .

Bugs Bunny singing Dixie
Mickey Mouse as Uncle Tom
Mickey (always) in minstrel gloves
Jerry of Tom-and-Jerry dipped in ink

a woman caller said two black men

no the woman said two men were seen

when the cop came said the black were no

said almost nothing she hadn't seen

the one inside the white cop said

was angry hostile a black man who

asked for the white cop's didn't know

if he'd been white was not the black

the woman didn't say he was

disorderly said the handcuffs what

happens to black the arrested said

in America in New England in

my city breaking into his own house

The White Tree was green, shady
oak in the schoolyard for whites
only, until a black student sat
there and three nooses were hung
from its branches the next day

three nooses   white tree

Three white students were caught
and suspended for three days, black
students sat by the tree to protest, one
black was beaten by whites, a white
man threatened others with a gun

three students   three days

Finally six black students "punched
and kicked" a white student, one
with a sneaker called a "deadly weapon"
at the trial where he was sentenced
to 22 years for attempted murder

one shoe   22 years

10,000 people, mostly black,
came to town as thousands of white
people had gone to similar towns
to see nooses hung from trees
with black bodies years before

white-trunked nightmare tree

The case was retried, but cases
were still pending when nooses began
to appear everywhere: a professor's
door, a police station locker, a highway
department, a sanitation garage

those white doors   those white walls

But back in the little town
of Jena, the white tree
was cut down

a white-trunked white-
limbed white-leafed tree

white petals sepals white
stamens pistils bees inside

a white woman pure
white body skin hair

white eyes white
lips nipples blood

white grass for the white
stones of this white dream

a majority white   means

of defending   against non-

only sensible   all whites

welcome   separate state

separation   of the strictest

Christian   more children

bring them up   fulfill

our God-given   white

future homeland   violent

third reich   war and blood

shed   racial revolution pan

Aryan   white against

[39]

Black people can turn white!

[see *vitiligo*]

Black people can *be* white!

[see *albino*]

White people can turn black!

[see *miscegenation, laws against*]

so they measured brain space lined up skulls
invented a second creation for after-the-flood

so they measured test scores not the test
told *us* that *we* must reproduce

told *them* to go back home

because black people could brown

people could brown people could

yellow people could brown people

could white people could disappear!

because   people could

[40]

White clouds draped with black rain in the

Hail rolling like beads from a broken

Snow coming frost on our

Fog so thick

When it isn't clear we

Gray clouds we walk in white weather

sleet   sheet   hail   shot

bead   eye   shut   my

couldn't see a

could dis-

appear in snow

Poe's Pym's sea

of milk white

ashes vapor

curtain split

to chasmed un-

colored human

form snow

man of nothing

is not there that

is the an-

nihilating

absence The

Whiteness of

the made our own

self the white Whale

my white I've said my
baby bed underwear tub
toilet washing machine
whatever got rid of dirt my
wedding dress veil what-
ever could hide X sheets
bleached coffin lined
against the dark dirt
banned when we started
to buy underwear in colors
even black white was on
its way out of cover over

o   o   o   o   o

November 4, 2008

[43]

Today the train *too fast*
they said *too soon* they
said *not yet* they said

to Washington right
now: to the White
House on the train

On his way to the Capitol largely built by slaves
who baked bricks, cut, laid stone—
                                        on his way
to stand before the Mall where slaves were held
in pens and sold—
                        on his way to the White
House partly built by slaves, where another
resident, after his Proclamation, wrote:
If slavery is not wrong, nothing is wrong

One hundred years later   King said
*Now is the time   We can never
be satisfied as long as*   he

dreamed: *every valley
exalted*   all these years until
not an end   they said   *a beginning*

[44]

when an other, a one
you've capitalized upon,
rightly decides to capitalize

itself, should you capitalize
yourself as well as the other
to remind yourself you have

what you've never fully
acknowledged: a race, a place
in an unbalanced history,

which you've used to your great
advantage, which is what
it means to capitalize,

which is what you're trying not
to do, so you keep lowercasing
yourself, but now you can't decide

what to do about the others: you
wonder whether someday we
might capitalize no one, nothing at all

[45]

although my father although
my mother although we rarely
although we whispered

although the silence although
the absence although even now
some TV books not to mention

radio websites new militias hate
groups raging against our socialist-
communist-fascist although but still:

our textbooks now our museums
mostly our college literature
courses even our crayons not

to mention our young president
who could scarcely have been
imagined when we when I—

and although I've gone back
and filled in some blanks
I'm still learning this un-

learning untying
the knot of *Yes but* re-
writing this   *Yes*   Yes

ACKNOWLEDGMENTS

I am grateful to the Radcliffe Institute for Advanced Study for its support of 40 Concord Avenue (and especially to Gail Mazur and Judy Vichniac) and to Cornell University (and especially to Alice Fulton) for the space and time that allowed much of this book to be researched, pondered, and written.

My thanks as well to Ed Ochester and to the many friends and listeners, too numerous to mention, who read and responded to this work while it was being written.

The sources I read or consulted are also too numerous to mention: the writing of *White Papers* included a process of self-education that often became its own end. But the following were essential for specific sections, and in many cases influenced me in more general ways as well:

On slavery in New England: Anne Farrow, Joel Lang, and Jenifer Frank, *Complicity: How the North Promoted, Prolonged, and Profited from Slavery* (2005); Winthrop D. Jordan, *White Over Black: American Attitudes Toward the Negro, 1550–1812* (1968); Joanne Pope Melish, *Disowning Slavery: Gradual Emancipation and "Race" in New England, 1780–1860* (1998); and W. E. B. DuBois, *The Suppression of the African Slave-Trade to the United States of America, 1638–1870* (1896). The italicized words in [14] are from Joseph Conrad, *Heart of Darkness* (1899, 1902).

On race in Iowa: Dorothy Schwieder, *Iowa: The Middle Land* (1996); *Iowa Pathways* (iptv.org/iowapathways); and "The Rosa Parks of Iowa," roxanneconlinlaw.com.

On the history of whiteness: Theodore W. Allen, *The Invention of the White Race*, vols. 1 and 2 (1994, 1997); Noel Ignatiev, *How the Irish Became White* (1995); Toni Morrison,

Playing in the Dark: Whiteness and the Literary Imagination (1992); David R. Roediger, *The Wages of Whiteness: Race and the Making of the American Working Class* (1991). Nell Irvin Painter's *The History of White People* (2010), published after I completed this collection, is an important discussion of this subject.

On Asian wars: the quote in the second section of [26] is from a government film produced in defense of the World War II internment of Japanese Americans; see archive .org/details/Japanese1943. Details about Operation Speedy Express are from *The Nation* (December 1, 2008).

On "white money": John W. Jones, *Confederate Currency: The Color of Money* (2002).

On white privilege: Peggy McIntosh, "White Privilege: Unpacking the Invisible Knapsack" (1989), in Paula S. Rothenberg, ed., *White Privilege: Essential Readings on the Other Side of Racism* (2004), and also, in a shorter version, on various websites. See other essays in Rothenberg as well.

On sundown towns: James W. Loewen, *Sundown Towns: A Hidden Dimension of American Racism* (2005).

On Ruby Berkley Goodwin: in addition to her own *It's Good to Be Black* (1953), Jill Watts, *Hattie McDaniel: Black Ambition, White Hollywood* (2005) and the online *Contemporary Authors* entry for Goodwin.

On minstrelsy: most centrally, Eric Lott, *Love and Theft: Blackface Minstrelsy and the American Working Class* (1993). Also Susan Gubar, *Racechanges: White Skin, Black Face in American Culture* (1997), and Roediger, cited above, as well as

the films listed in the fifth and seventh sections of [36].
Most of the film versions of *Uncle Tom's Cabin* are available at:
utc.iath.virginia.edu/onstage/films/fihp.html.

Unnumbered sections on pp. 18 and 56 quote, respectively,
Johnny Gruelle, *Beloved Belindy* (originally 1926), and the
following websites: stormfront.org, crusader.net/resources/
election.html, aryan-nations.org.

The events referenced in [37] occurred in 2009 in
Cambridge, Massachusetts; those referenced in [38]
occurred in 2006–2007 in Jena, Louisiana.

Finally, I would like to thank the editors of the following
publications, in which some sections of this book first
appeared, often with different numbers: *Ancora Imparo, AWP
Chronicle, Connotation Press, Consequence, Copper Nickel, Crab
Orchard Review, 5 AM, Harvard Review, Iowa Review, The
Journal, Massachusetts Review, Michigan Quarterly Review, The
Midwest Quarterly, Pleiades, Ploughshares, Poetry International,
Poets.org, Prairie Schooner, Solstice, Tidal Basin Review,* and
Witness.